My Mom and Dad Are Getting a Divorce

for children, parents, teachers, counselors, and attorneys

By

Florence Bienenfeld, Ph.D., M.F.T.

ISBN: 1-4033-4998-3 (e-book)
ISBN: 1-4033-4999-1 (Paperback)

Library of Congress Control Number: 2002093064

Printed in the United States of America
Bloomington, IN

1stBooks – rev 12/6/02

Author
Florence Bienenfeld, Ph.D., M.F.T.

Family Counselor/Mediator and author of <u>Helping Your Child Through Your Divorce</u>, <u>Child Custody Mediation</u>, and <u>Do It Yourself Conflict Resolution for Couples</u>. Former Senior Counselor and Mediator for Family Court Services, Superior Court of California, County of Los Angeles.

Illustrator
Art Scott, B.E.

Former Producer and Vice President, Hanna-Barbera Productions

Consultant
Meyer Elkin, M.S.W.

Former Director, Family Court Services, Superior Court of California, County of Los Angeles; Co-founder and Past President, Association of Family Conciliation Courts; Editor, Conciliation Courts Review

Endorsed by

The Association of Family Conciliation Courts
6515 Grand Teton Plaza, Suite 210
Madison, Wisconsin 53719

The Association of Family Conciliation Courts (A.F.C.C.) is an international non-profit organization that promotes and supports court-counseling services and programs for divorcing families.

Library of Congress Cataloging in Publication Data

Bienenfeld, Florence.
My mom and dad are getting a divorce.

SUMMARY: Examines a young girl and boy's feelings about their parents'
divorce and how they and their parents cope with these emotions. Includes
counseling guides for parents, teachers, counselors and attorneys.

1. Divorce — United States — Juvenile literature. 2. Children of divorced
parents — United States — Juvenile literature. [1. Divorce] II. Title.

Acknowledgements

The author wishes to express her appreciation to the many colleagues, friends, and professionals in the field who offered guidance and support, as well as to her family. Special thanks go to the late Meyer Elkin, former Director of Family Court Services, Superior Court of California, County of Los Angeles, who generously served as consultant on this book.

The following notable people gave the manuscript very favorable reviews: Carl A. Whitaker, M.D., former Professor of Psychiatry, University of Wisconsin Medical School; C. Ray Fowler, Ph.D., former Executive Director, American Association of Marriage and Family Therapists; Saul L. Brown, M.D., former Director, Department of Psychiatry, Cedars-Sinai Medical Center; Peggy Conkling, former Vice President – Public Relations, Parents Without Partners, Inc.

The author is eternally grateful to the late Art Scott, former Vice President of Hanna-Barbera Productions, who generously donated his time and talents to personally do all of the illustrations for <u>My Mom and Dad Are Getting a Divorce</u>, without whose dedication and enthusiasm this book would not have become a reality.

The author values the years she worked at the Family Court Services, Superior Court of California, County of Los Angeles and wishes to thank the entire staff and the thousands of families she counseled. <u>My Mom and Dad Are Getting a Divorce</u> was an outgrowth of her experience on a daily basis of seeing how so many children were being tormented by the divorce and in need of relief and healing.

The author wishes to commend and thank The Association of Family Conciliation Courts for their programs and support of court-counseling services for divorcing families. A portion of the author's royalties from this book is being donated to A.F.C.C. Many thanks to A.F.C.C. Co-Chairs of Publication Committee: Phil Bushard, Past-President of A.F.C.C., Director of Family Mediation Program, Washoe County, Nevada and Doneldon Dennis, Past Board Member of A.F.C.C., Supervisor, Hennepin County Family Court Services, Minnesota for their fine suggestions used in the Epilogue For Parents of this book.

Acknowledgements and many thanks also go to Terrie Barna, A.S.A.P. Word Processing, for her outstanding secretarial support. And, to Dan Heise and Niccole Powers at 1stBooks Library for their attentive and responsive service.

Last but not least, the author wishes to thank her dear husband, Mickey, her three wonderful children and five grandchildren for their love and support. Never did she think when she wrote this book that she would be reading it to her own grandchildren to ease their pain of divorce, but she did.

Dedication

To the millions of children, moms, and dads who are going through, or who have gone through, the crisis of separation and divorce.

LOS ANGELES TIMES BOOK REVIEW

My Mom and Dad Are Getting a Divorce by Florence Bienenfeld, is more than just another children's book on divorce. It's also a guide for divorcing parents who need help handling the emotional turmoil that afflicts them as well as the kids. The colorfully illustrated children's story — an engaging dialogue between a boy and a girl who compare their experiences as children of divorce — is accompanied by a page-by-page commentary offering sensible advice to parents. As a result, this modest, unpretentious book amounts to a remarkable resource.

The wisdom, compassion and common sense that fill the pages of "My Mom and Dad Are Getting a Divorce" are drawn from the rich personal experience of Florence Bienenfeld, who served as a Senior Marriage and Family Counselor of the Conciliation Court of Los Angeles County Superior Court. Illustrations by Hanna-Barbera producer Arthur Scott help young readers grasp feelings that they may not be able to express openly. Above all, Bienenfeld's annotations allow parents to understand and cope with the complex problems that arise from even the most cordial divorce.

Preface

This book is for children and parents, as well as professionals working with divorcing families. It focuses on the feelings young children have when their parents divorce. It tells "how it is" for two fictional characters, Amy and Dan. At the same time, the book describes the feelings of millions of real children who experience separation and divorce.

The purpose of the book is to help children acknowledge, deal with and communicate the feelings of sadness, loss, hurt, anger, guilt, helplessness, and fear triggered by the divorce. The book demonstrates in story form how parents can be helpful and reassuring. The ways Amy's parents reassure her in the story and the commentaries for parents in the Appendix can serve as a guide to parents.

This book is not designed to make parents feel guilty about getting a divorce. Rather, its purpose is to help parents become aware of what their children are experiencing and how they can minimize the hurt. Regrettably, the hurt that children suffer is too often ignored in our society.

My Mom and Dad Are Getting a Divorce is intended for children four through twelve years of age. The book can be read to young children. Children in the second through sixth grades can either read it by themselves or with parents. The book can also be used by elementary and preschool teachers to stimulate discussion about divorce. Further, the book can be used as a resource for parenthood and occupational child-care courses in high school and college.

A child's adjustment to separation and divorce depends on what parents do or say. The adjustment can be made easier or more difficult. This book is designed to help both parents and children deal more effectively with divorce, so that they can regain their equilibrium and use the crisis to grow.

MY MOM AND DAD ARE GETTING A DIVORCE

For Children 4 to 12

A MESSAGE FOR PARENTS TEACHERS AND COUNSELORS

Re: use of this children's book

The author, Florence Bienenfeld, suggests that young children, ages 4, 5, 6, 7, and even 8 years old, be read to. Afterwards, they may enjoy looking at pictures on their own. Children third grade and up can read this book by themselves or with a parent, teacher, or counselor.

They told me they're sorry about the divorce. They wish we could all live together, but we can't!

Epilogue for Parents

Divorce is a crisis for the entire family. The recovery takes time. The whole family must go through various stages to mourn the loss of a relationship. Both adults and children go through stages of mourning ranging from disbelief, bargaining, anger, rage, fear, anxiety, sadness, and depression to the final stage of acceptance. During this difficult period, parents are often so upset that they have difficulty setting aside their anger to cooperate as parents about their children. Children can survive the divorce, but they can't heal being involved in an ongoing tug-of-war between their parents or losing one of their parents as result of the divorce. Cooperation is the key to helping children survive divorce.

It's never too late to begin a new approach. When cooperation doesn't seem possible, or when parents find themselves too upset to be supportive to their children, counseling can be helpful. Some communities provide family counseling through the Conciliation or Family Court Services at no cost. Family Service Agencies and Professional Counseling Associations are listed in the yellow pages of the telephone directory under the heading, *Marriage and Family Counselors.* You can also write to the American Association of Marriage and Family Therapy, 1133 15th Street NW, Washington, DC 20005.

For better or worse, children survive divorce but, some never recover from the emotional scars by parents who remain in conflict. These scars handicap many of them for life from forming deep, lasting relationships in adult life. This need not happen. The solution is *cooperation.* Cooperation between parents is possible even when the marriage relationship wasn't a good one.

Cooperation means

- settling on a workable parenting plan that gives children access with both parents
- keeping ongoing contact with the children so they don't feel rejected or abandoned
- preparing the children beforehand for the separation, whenever possible
- reassuring children that they can still count on both parents
- rarely canceling plans with children or rescheduling at the last minute
- each parent establishing a home for the children with a place for their clothes, toys, etc.
- maintaining telephone contact with the children
- encouraging the children's telephone access with both parents
- having children ready on time for the other parent
- being home to receive the children on time
- picking the children up and dropping them off on time
- calling the other parent when it is necessary to be late
- communicating openly about serious matters concerning the children.
- not using the children to get information about the other parent
- not trying to control the other parent
- not using the children to carry angry messages back and forth
- not using the children to deliver child support payments
- not arguing in front of the children
- not speaking derogatorily about the other parent
- not asking the children with whom they want to live
- not pressuring or expecting the children to take sides
- not using the children as weapons to hurt the other parent

Cooperation creates the kind of environment in which children feel safe, satisfied, and loved.

Appendices

I. <u>My Mom And Dad Are Getting A Divorce</u>: Page-by-Page Comments for Parents, Teachers, Counselors, and Attorneys.

II. How Children Experience Custody Disputes

III. Ten Commandments for Divorcing Parents

IV. Creating a Conflict-Free Zone for Your Child

V. Basic Concepts Divorcing Parents Need to Know

VI. Suggested Guidelines for Parents

VII. Characteristics of a Healthy Reconstructed Family After Divorce

VIII. How Mediation Can Help

IX. Concepts Discussed in Mediation

X. Difficult Situations and Corresponding Concepts and Strategies

XI. Creating a Closer Relationship with Your Child

Florence Bienenfeld

Appendix I

MY MOM AND DAD ARE GETTING A DIVORCE

Page-by-Page Comments for
Parents, Teachers, Counselors, and Attorneys

Page 1: A message to parents, teachers, and counselors suggests how to use this book with various age children.

Pages 2 & 3: Amy doesn't want to play just now. Deep feelings of sadness and loss come up for most children when their parents divorce.

Pages 4 & 5: Amy tells her friends the sad news. Most children take divorce very hard. Since they are so dependent on parents, a divorce becomes a serious threat to their security.

Pages 6 & 7: Amy explains divorce to her friend in the only way she knows how. What divorce means to most children is that parents don't want to live together anymore.

Pages 8 & 9: Amy doesn't understand why her parents don't want to live together or why her father is leaving the home. Children don't really understand adult problems. They are confused and bewildered. Sometimes they believe that the parent who stays with them loves them more than the one who leaves, which is often not the case.

Parents should give children a simple reason for the divorce and spare children all the details. Parents cause children great emotional pain when they try to pressure the children to take sides by blaming the other parent or talking against the other parent. Children need to look up to both parents.

Pages 10 & 11: Amy actually pleads with her father not to go. Small children have only their parents to cling to. They become frightened when parents leave them, even for an evening. They should be told, and helped to believe and feel, that mom and dad both still love them and have every intention of continuing to see them and take care of them, even though they live apart.

Pages 12 & 13: Amy feels angry at her father for leaving her. It doesn't matter to a child what the parent's reason is for leaving. Even when a parent dies, children feel rejected and angry. Sometimes they also become angry with the parent who stays because that parent won't bring the other parent back.

Pages 14 & 15: Fortunately, Amy's father tells her he will see her often. A parental plan should be arranged before the separation or as soon as possible after the separation. Otherwise, some children believe they will never see the other parent again.

It is not necessary or even desirable for a parent to spend a lot of money on taking children places or buying them presents. The important thing is to spend pleasant times together. It's what you do with them — not buy for them — that counts.

Pages 16 & 17: Dan tells Amy his parents are divorced and he lives with his mother. With the incidence of divorce at over one million families each year in the United States, most children have some friends whose parents are divorced. Many children live with their mothers and see their fathers on weekends; however, there is a growing trend toward more fathers getting involved in child rearing and toward co-parenting or joint custody arrangements. Children tend to do best when both parents remain involved following the divorce.

Pages 18 & 19: Dan remembers the arguments his parents had. Such memories are very painful for children. Children become frightened and insecure when they see parents argue or lose control.

Scenes should be avoided in the presence of the children. Children also feel uncomfortable when they sense tension between parents.

Pages 20 & 21: Dan tells Amy he's happy when he gets to see his father. Some children feel rejected, angry, and unloved when they don't see a parent regularly. Some children come to believe they're not worth loving. These feelings can remain with them throughout life if parents don't cooperate and don't arrange a plan that gives children access to both parents.

Pages 22 & 23: Dan tells Amy his parents still argue when his father comes to pick him up. Parents don't have to like each other or live together. The only thing they have to do now is to be parents. The more parents cooperate and create a harmonious environment for the children, the easier it is on the children. When parents continue to hassle and argue, they make their children's lives bitter.

Pages 24 & 25: Dan sees how friendly his friend's parents are and wishes his parents would be friendly, too. Most children wish their parents would get along. When parents don't get along, the children are caught in the middle.

Pages 26 & 27: Dan tells Amy his mother is getting married again. Some children resist loving step-parents because they feel they're being disloyal to their real father or mother. When children are told it's okay to love all the people in their lives who are good and kind to them, a burden of guilt is lifted off of them.

Pages 28 & 29: Amy finds comfort in knowing she'll have a home with each of her parents. Whenever possible, parents should try to provide a bed, place for toys, some clothing, toothbrush, hairbrush, desk or place to study, books, etc., for the children so they can feel at home in both places, not like a visitor.

Pages 30 & 31: Amy's father told her he wouldn't be living far away. Many children feel anxious and out of touch when a parent moves out of the home. They should be taken to the parent's new place as soon as possible and given the new telephone number.

Pages 32 & 33: Amy wishes her father would come home again. Children tend to hold onto the dream that their parents will get back together some day. Some cling to this dream for years, even after one or both parents remarry.

Pages 34 & 35: Amy's parents let her know they won't be getting back together again. This honesty helps children accept the divorce as a reality and aids them in adjusting to their new life.

Pages 36 through 41: Amy, like many real children, tends to blame herself for what has happened. Amy thinks about some of the "bad" things she did and feels guilty. She thinks, "If only I had been a better kid, maybe they wouldn't be getting a divorce." Amy's parents let her know it wasn't her fault. A few simple, reassuring words can help relieve a lot of guilt and misery.

Pages 42 & 43: Amy is frightened. Children worry about what will become of them and who will take care of them. They sometimes fear the remaining parent may "divorce" them, also, if they don't mind. Some children test parents to see how far they can go. They need to be told that they will be taken care of no matter what happens between mom and dad. Parents should avoid telling children they'll be sent to live with the other parent as a punishment. This only intensifies their insecurity.

Pages 44 & 45: Amy must face many new adjustments: a new house, neighborhood, school, friends, baby sitters, in addition to the big changes in her family situation. All these changes can be overwhelming, even for parents. The fewer changes the first year, the better.

Pages 46 & 47: Amy tells Dan her mother is looking for a job. Children worry about who is going to take care of them.

Pages 48 & 49: Dan tells Amy his mother works. Most children adjust well to their mother working as long as the quality of care provided for them is good, and as long as the mother-child relationship continues to be loving and nurturing.

Pages 50 & 51: Dan tells Amy about his child-care center. Licensed day-care centers and licensed child-care centers are located in most communities, and listed in telephone yellow pages under Day-Care-Child, Baby Sitters, Schools-Preschools and Kindergarten, or Social Service Organizations.

Pages 52 & 53: Amy wonders why her parents have to divorce. It can be helpful for parents to take the time to find out delicately from each child separately what they think caused the divorce, how they feel about the divorce, and what they're most worried about now. This should be a time for the parent to listen and reassure children, not a time for arguing them out of their feelings, or telling them who's right and who's wrong. Children should be encouraged to remain neutral and not take sides.

Pages 54 & 55: Amy feels powerless and helpless to do anything about the divorce. Children feel an almost overwhelming sense of powerlessness and helplessness. The adults in their lives make all the moves; they have to follow along.

Pages 56 & 57: Amy's parents did a good job of reassuring her. Children need to hear this from parents, especially at a time like this.

Pages 58 & 59: Amy's parents told her they're sorry about the divorce. Parents should let their children know they really care and wish they could have kept the family together.

Pages 60 & 61: Amy's parents tell her they understand how hard it is for her now. They also reassure her that soon she and they will feel better.

Children don't know what to expect. It is helpful if parents acknowledge how difficult this time is for them, too, and still offer children some feeling of optimism for the future.

Pages 62 & 63: Amy comes to the realization that she hasn't lost her parents after all. This is the one thing that can help children feel better. It takes a lot of reassurance, understanding, courage, and love to help children feel secure again.

Pages 64 & 65: Now Amy can play. She expressed many feelings to her friend Dan. She begins to believe maybe life can be okay after all. Children need to work through these feelings with some caring person, preferably a parent; if not a parent, perhaps a counselor could be of help.

For better or worse, children survive divorce. If they feel rejected or abandoned, they can become bitter and resolve never to love anyone ever again. This reluctance to love deeply can follow them into adulthood and keep them from forming lasting, deep love relationships. This need never happen if parents cooperate and help their children know and feel they still have two parents they can depend on. Out of this trust can blossom a full capacity to love and a good chance for a happy life.

<u>Appendix II</u>

HOW CHILDREN EXPERIENCE CUSTODY DISPUTES

Children suffer a lot when parents will not cooperate, or when they lose contact with one parent as a result of the divorce. Even when children enjoy a close relationship with one of their parents, they tend to suffer from lowered self-esteem if they have infrequent contact with, or feel rejected by, the other parent. Children in the middle of parental conflicts often feel confused, anxious, angry, frustrated, guilty, sad, depressed, hopeless, and powerless.

some quotations from children's interviews

Children's interviews disclose some of the pain they experience. One fourteen-year-old boy whose parents divorced when he was five said, "I felt like an attorney. My mother would tell me one thing and my father would tell me another. I didn't know who was right. I finally decided my mother was right." He explained that once he took sides with his mother, he did not want to see his father anymore.

"I wish I was never born," said a sensitive twelve-year-old girl whose parents divorced when she was two, "because they're fighting over me."

One sad eight-year-old boy whose parents "kidnapped" him from each other since they separated a year ago said, "I wish I could go away where nice people take care of children."

"My daddy told me my mother left us because she didn't love us anymore," said an angry nine-year-old girl. By the time her parents ended up in court, she did not want to see her mother anymore.

A confused five-year-old boy who had not seen his father for a year and a half said, "I thought I'd never see my daddy again. I didn't know why he never came to see me." He had no way of knowing that his mother had kept him in hiding. It had taken his father a year and a half to find him.

77

children's drawings

Some children in custody battles express their agony in drawings. One eleven-year-old boy drew himself as a small stick figure hanging on a ladder that was stretched between two hills. He labeled the void underneath him as "The Pits." On one hill he wrote, "I love you, Dad. I'll buy you a motorcycle." On the other hill he wrote, "I love you too, Mom. Come. We'll have a lot of fun."

His nine-year-old sister drew a row of five big daisies. She named each daisy. The two daisies on the left she colored orange. She labeled one "Mommy" and labeled the other one with her stepfather's name. The two daisies on the right she colored purple: one was labeled "Daddy"; the other was labeled with her stepmother's name. The center daisy she labeled "Me." This one was half orange and half purple. Fortunately, the parents of these two children were willing to work out a shared custody parenting plan that gave the children access to both parents. These children got their wish.

One morning another eight-year-old girl drew a sad-faced girl standing in a rainstorm. Underneath her drawing she wrote, "This is how I feel." During the family conference, I hung it on the wall. By noon she was jumping with joy and relief because her parents had reached an amicable agreement.

pain, conflict, and behavior

Children express their inner pain and conflict in various ways. Some children bottle up their feelings about divorce. Some act out their aggression. Others are quiet and withdrawn. Especially when parents keep the battle going or make visitation difficult, children feel alone with their pain. They do not have the parental help they need to complete the mourning process and to recover and heal from the divorce.

Even when children appear to be coping at the time, the damage can surface later in their lives. Feelings that are not resolved persist or become more intense and can cause problems later.

where to find help[*]

When parents find that they are too upset to focus on their children's needs — especially when children are exhibiting very hostile, aggressive, withdrawn, or regressive behavior — they should seek family counseling.

When parents are not able to reach an agreement regarding their children, they can find help through private divorce counselors, mediators, and agencies providing these services. These resources are available in most communities. For information regarding counseling and mediation services contact the following resources: local courthouses, Conciliation Courts and Family Court Services; The Association of Family Conciliation Courts, 6515 Grand Teton, Suite 210, Madison, WI 53719, (608) 664-3750, www.afccnet.org, (provides specific contact information for your area at no charge); the American Association of Marriage and Family Therapists, 1133 15th Street NW, Suite 300, Washington, DC 20005, (202) 452-0109; County Mental Health agencies; and telephone directory yellow pages listed under Crisis Intervention Services, Divorce Services, Marriage and Family Therapists, Mental Health Services, Parents Guidance Instruction, Psychologists, Psychotherapists, Psychiatrists, Social Services Organizations and Mediation Services.

---

[*] Excerpts from <u>Child Custody Mediation</u> by Florence Bienenfeld, Ph.D., 1stBooks Library, 2002, 1-888-280-7715 or www.1stbooks.com or Amazon.com.

<u>Appendix III</u>

TEN COMMANDMENTS FOR DIVORCING PARENTS

Below are ten guidelines that may help you establish a conflict-free zone. These suggestions are a code of conduct, a positive guide on how to treat the other parent. If you follow them, your child will be much less likely to be caught in the crossfire of continual parental conflict.

Each suggestion touches on a different aspect of the parental relationship. The first suggestion lays the groundwork for establishing a parental relationship after separation or divorce. The second and sixth suggestions are about the need to respect the other parent's rights to privacy and to private time with the child. The third, fourth, and fifth call on parents to avoid critical and hostile interactions. The last four suggestions encourage trust and cooperation and assist in developing positive problem-solving skills.

If at times following these guidelines is difficult, remember this: When you treat the other parent with respect, you are doing it for your child and for yourself, *not* for the other parent.

1. Shift gears from being marriage partners to being parent partners.

2. Settle disagreements through give-and-take and compromise, and respect individual differences.

3. Treat the other parent with respect, and avoid making derogatory statements about the other parent in the presence of your child.

4. Avoid arguments, scenes, threats, fights, and violence, especially when your children are present.

5. Don't be overly critical of or try to control the other parent.

6. Avoid pressuring the other parent about getting back together, and respect the other parent's privacy.

7. Don't sacrifice your child over money.

8. Make child-support payments on time.

9. Gain the other parent's trust by keeping your agreements and promises.

10. Accept the facts that the other parent has the right to spend time with the children, and that your children have the right to a relationship with the other parent.

Excerpts from <u>Helping Your Child Through Your Divorce</u> by Florence Bienenfeld, Ph.D., Hunter House, 1995, 1-800-266-5592 or www.HunterHouse.com or Amazon.com

Appendix IV

CREATING A CONFLICT-FREE ZONE FOR YOUR CHILD

If children are to succeed after divorce, they must be protected from parental conflict and allowed to enjoy close relationships with both parents. Despite pain, resentment, and disagreements, it is possible for divorced parents to surround their children with a "conflict-free" zone.

The diagram below shows a child in a small circle, the conflict-free zone. It is surrounded by a larger circle, the parental conflict zone. The space between the two circles is a buffer zone between the child and the parental conflict.

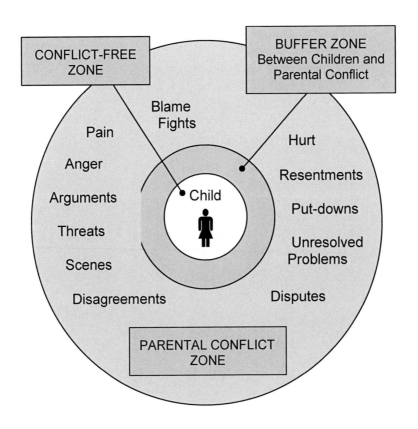

Excerpts from <u>Helping Your Child Through Your Divorce</u> by Florence Bienenfeld, Ph.D., Hunter House, 1995, 1-800-266-5592 or www.HunterHouse.com or Amazon.com

<u>Appendix V</u>

BASIC CONCEPTS DIVORCING PARENTS NEED TO KNOW

1. Children need to feel loved and cared about by both parents.

2. Even if the child has a close and loving relationship with one parent, if the child doesn't also experience a satisfying relationship with the other parent, the child's self-esteem tends to suffer.

3. Children need to be protected from parental conflict, arguments, and violence.

4. Children need to be protected from the pressure of having to choose where they want to live.

5. Children need to be given the right to a relationship with both parents, and significant time with both.

6. Children need freedom to express concerns and feelings, even negative ones.

7. Children need reasonable limits set for their behavior, and sufficient warning before disciplinary action is taken.

8. Children need reassurance they will continue to be cared for.

9. Children need to be cared for by kind and caring people, and protected from emotional, physical, and sexual abuse.

10. Divorce is devastating for children but they can recover and do well <u>if</u> their parents work together to help the child.

11. Even if parents don't like each other they can learn to work together for the good of the child. They are no longer <u>marriage partners</u>, but they are still <u>parent partners</u>.

12. Children tend to do best after separation and divorce when both parents are involved in their lines. The children who would tend to do worst are those who are exposed to continual parental conflict, and those who lose a parent as a result of the divorce. Even sporadic visits are better for a child than no visits.

13. When parents can't work things out between themselves — help is available. Divorce mediation is a powerful process. A mediator is a neutral third party who helps parents discuss issues regarding the children and explore ways of resolving differences. Through mediation many parents are able to reach an agreement and avoid a costly court battle.

14. Court litigation over the child custody issues should be a last resort, because it leads to more dissatisfaction and hostility between parents, and usually results in more problems for children.

15. There are some warning signs of a child in trouble: anxiety, depression, bedwetting, eating or sleeping disorders, school problems, overaggressive behavior, alcohol or drug abuse, and other symptoms that persist. If this occurs parents should seek help before the child sustains lasting psychological damage.

16. Children need protection and reassurance from both parents. It is up to parents to create a safe and nurturing environment for their children after divorce.

17. It's not too late to change your behavior and attitudes to help your child. Children are resilient and can heal quickly once their situation is improved. The longer the child is exposed to parental conflict or feelings of abandonment, the greater the likelihood for serious psychological damage to occur.

Appendix VI

SUGGESTED GUIDELINES FOR PARENTS

Parents can create a safer, more secure and harmonious environment for their children by following these suggested guidelines:

1. Refrain from saying anything of a derogatory nature about the other parent in the presence of the child(ren).

2. Refrain from bringing up past grievances regarding the other parent to the child(ren).

3. Refrain from discussing financial and legal issues and disputes with the child(ren).

4. Refrain from saying anything which might discourage the child(ren) from spending time with the other parent, and from pressuring the child(ren) to take sides against the other parent.

5. Be willing to share the children with the other parent, and work out a parenting plan as soon as possible after the separation.

6. Be willing to cooperate and communicate with the other parent regarding the children.

7. Encourage the children to have a close relationship with both parents, stepparents, and grandparents.

8. Focus on the present and on the children's needs instead of on the past. Focusing on the past is self-defeating and can only harm both parent and child.

9. Spend as much time as possible with the child(ren) during the time you are responsible for them.

10. Carefully avoid scheduling or arranging activities for the child(ren) which are likely to conflict with any time period allocated to the other parent.

11. In the event a parent is unable to keep his or her scheduled arrangements with the child(ren) on a given occasion, that parent should notify the other parent at the earliest possible opportunity.

12. Arrange ahead of time for both parents to be authorized in writing to take any and all actions necessary to protect the health and welfare of the child(ren) in case of emergency.

13. Keep the other parent advised at all times of your current residence address, telephone numbers (home and work), your child(ren)'s school or child care facility, and the location where your child(ren) will be spending any extended period of time (four days or more). This information is not to be used for the purpose of harassing or annoying each other in any way.

14. Since it is both frightening and damaging for children to be exposed to violence and parental conflict, avoid arguments, fights, and threats in the presence of the child(ren).

15. Since child(ren) need to be able to depend on and to trust both parents, keep the agreements and promises you have made to the other parent and to your child(ren). This means being reliable about keeping appointments and schedules, being prompt, and not making promises to children that you cannot keep.

16. Cooperate fully, not only in carrying out the written terms of your court order or agreement, but in living up to the underlying spirit of the order as well.

17. For your child(ren)'s sake, make a special effort to set aside your personal feelings toward the other parent and maintain an attitude of respect, tolerance, flexibility, and good faith.

<u>Appendix VII</u>

CHARACTERISTICS OF A HEALTHY RECONSTRUCTED FAMILY AFTER DIVORCE

After divorce the restructured family can be whole and healthy. The list of characteristics below can serve as a guide and model for parents to strive for

1. Willingness on part of both parents to set past aside and focus on their children's needs.

2. Ability and willingness to communicate regarding their children.

3. Willingness to share time and responsibility for raising their children.

4. Willingness to respect the other parent's privacy and promote the other parent's relationship with the children.

5. Willingness to cooperate in crisis situations.

6. Willingness to seek help when needed.

Appendix VIII

HOW MEDIATION CAN HELP

In the mid-seventies, Conciliation Courts, Family Courts Services and mediation centers across the nation began providing mediation services for litigating parents. These centers were created to reduce the harmful effects of divorce on children and to ease congestion in the courts. As of January 1981, California mandated mediation in all contested custody and visitation disputes. Mediation is now becoming more widespread and available to families as an alternative to the adversary approach.

Custody and visitation mediation is already available in many areas of the United States and is continually reaching more people. Custody mediation is currently practiced in courts, mediation centers, and family therapy clinics. It is used by therapists and mediators in private practice, by attorneys, by interdisciplinary attorney-therapist teams, in churches, and so forth.

Mediation is increasingly popular as a means of resolving divorce and separation issues. It is quicker and cheaper than a court trial and it helps reduce the hostility and bitterness generated by the adversary system. Mediation encourages the disputants to resolve the issues rather than having the court decide for them. The voluntary choice of both parents to work together is what mediation relies upon. Since both parents actively participate in mediation, the settlement reached is often better suited to meet the family's needs than an order handed down by a judge from the bench.

The adversary process focuses on the past and encourages competition; mediation focuses on the future and encourages cooperation.

Mediation helps parents focus on their children's needs to reach a mutually agreeable settlement.

Separation and divorce are stress-filled times. Parents can easily allow themselves to lose control and be run by their emotions. They need to exercise great restraint to curtail hostile actions and remarks in their children's presence. It takes great courage for parents to take an honest look at some of their own attitudes and behaviors that are detrimental to children, such as thinking of the children as "mine" rather than "ours," keeping children away from the other parent to punish him or her, using children to gain a better financial settlement, controlling the time that children spend with the other parent, competing over children, not seeing children regularly, arguing or fighting in front of the children, asking children to choose sides or to say who they want to live with, snatching or keeping children away from the other parent, and continuing to bring up the past.

Some parents believe that the court can settle their problems regarding the children. This is rarely true. Instead, litigation can lead to more litigation, especially when parents are dissatisfied with what has been ordered in court. Some parents go back year after year, trying to resolve their conflicts. They do not realize that the courtroom is not the place to solve these disputes.

Some parents think they can win in court. Unless children end up with two involved parents, everyone loses. Children need two parents who are willing to cooperate, work together to raise them, and share time and responsibility for their care.

When parents cooperate after separation and divorce, children have a far better chance of healing from the divorce, of feeling more self-confident, of having higher self-esteem, and of feeling more reassured and less anxious about the future. The last thing they need is two parents fighting over them.

Besides benefiting children, mediation offers parents several important advantages as well. These include reduced frustration and hostility, less re-litigation, more satisfaction with the process, and substantial savings of both time and money.

Mediation is a powerful and effective process. It can help parents settle their differences at any stage of the divorce proceedings. However, the sooner parents avail themselves of it, the less possibility of the conflict escalating, and the less likelihood of trauma for the children. Many risks can be avoided when guidelines are established early on and parents feel reassured that they are not going to lose contact with their children.

An appointment for an exploratory session with a mediator can be arranged by attorneys or by the parents directly. When attorneys represent parents, parents can be instructed to discuss whatever agreements are reached during the mediation session with their attorneys before finalizing the agreements. Some mediators include attorneys in certain portions of the mediation process, such as at the beginning and/or toward the end. If an agreement is reached by parents with a mediator in a court setting, this agreement can be made into a legal court order. Agreements reached in noncourt settings can be written up as stipulations by attorneys and submitted to the court.

<u>Appendix IX</u>

CONCEPTS DISCUSSED IN MEDIATION

Concepts Discussed with Parents:

1. Divorce is a process, not a single event. Parents and children need time to go through its many phases.

2. Children are not a property or possession.

3. Custody and visitation disputes are very difficult and painful for children.

4. Children can heal from divorce when parents cooperate.

5. Children are depending upon parents to create a safe and harmonious environment for them.

6. Children need reassurance from both parents that they are still loved and will be taken care of.

7. Children need close and continuous contact with both parents.

8. Children need permission to love both parents and other important people in their lives, such as a stepparent or grandparents.

9. Children's education must not be interrupted.

10. Agreements should be kept by both parents so that they come to trust each other.

11. Parenting plans should be re-evaluated periodically and necessary changes made to meet children's and parents' changing needs.

12. Some flexibility is important. Parents should try to accommodate each other whenever possible to make *occasional* changes or special arrangements.

13. Both parents and children benefit when parents cooperate and work together.

Cooperation rather than competition is stressed in mediation. Parents are encouraged to focus on the present and future rather than on the past. I discuss the benefits that can be derived for themselves and, especially, for their children.

Concepts Discussed with Children:

1. Divorce is not the end of your family.

2. You are not losing one or both of your parents.

3. Although everyone is very upset right now, things should calm down soon.

4. This may take time.

5. The divorce is not your fault.

6. What happens is up to your parents. It is not your job to get your parents back together.

7. Parents are not leaving or divorcing you. they are leaving and/or divorcing each other.

8. Parents do not stop loving their children.

9. You will be cared for.

10. In most cases, children do have the chance to spend time with both parents.

Excerpts from <u>Child Custody Mediation</u> by Florence Bienenfeld, Ph.D., 1stBooks Library, 2002, 1-888-280-7715 or www.1stbooks.com or Amazon.com

<u>Appendix X</u>

DIFFICULT SITUATIONS AND CORRESPONDING CONCEPTS AND STRATEGIES

Parenting Situations, Positions, and Concerns	**Corresponding Parent Education Concepts and Strategies**
1. One or both parents want sole custody	Introduce discussion regarding joint-custody as an alternative to sole custody. *Concepts:* Parenting arrangements which afford children significant amounts of time with each parent are beneficial for children. Children tend to do best when both parents remain involved with the child. Sharing responsibility can benefit both parents and their children.
2. Financial issues are put before children's issues	*Concepts:* Financial issues can take a long time. They will get settled eventually. Children cannot be put on hold. They need a tolerable situation in the meantime. Children are not property. Issues regarding the children need to be settled first, and as soon as possible.
3. A child has lost contact with one parent	*Concepts:* For the child's sake contact should be re-established as soon as possible, and gradually if necessary, so as not to traumatize the child. Parental cooperation is paramount.

95

4. A child refuses to see a parent

Encourage parents to participate in family counseling with the child.

Concepts: No matter how close and loving a child's relationship is with one parent, unless the child also experiences a satisfaction relationship with the other parent, the child's self-esteem tends to suffer.

5. The child has witnessed physical and/or verbal abuse between parents

Caution parents about long-lasting negative consequences of children exposed to parental violence and conflict. Urge parents to protect their children from further reoccurrence of same.

Concept: Parents are models for their children. Parents should seek professional help for themselves and their children.

6. A parent is not seeing the children

Stress importance of that parent making a commitment regarding seeing the child regularly.

Concepts: Children do not understand adult problems. When a parent doesn't see them regularly, they feel rejected and abandoned. This can result in lowered self-esteem. Children need both parents.

7. One parent wants to withhold the children, or limit access

Concepts: Children have rights to know and have two parents. Children benefit from a close relationship with both parents. They suffer from feelings of rejection and abandonment when they are seen infrequently. This can result in low self-esteem. The more a parent resists letting the children have contact with the other parent, the more they will want to. A possessive attitude can backfire. A child's time with the other parent should be respected.

8. A parent is critical of the other parent's lifestyle or parenting style

Concepts: It is important for children to learn to respect individual differences. Parents are models for teaching this value. Trying to control the other parent or change the other parent is self-defeating. There are certain things a parent can't control. A child should be allowed to have his or her own relationship with the other parent.

9. One parent is very angry or hostile toward the other parent

Concepts: Both parents had a part in creating what happened during the marriage, and how their relationship developed and ended up. Seeing oneself as victim keeps a person stuck in the past. The anger keeps going and the person stops growing.

10. One or both parents make derogatory remarks regarding the other parent in front of the children

Concepts: Children need to be protected from parental conflict. They have a need to look up to both parents. This behavior is damaging for children.

11. A parent says a child is too young to go

Concepts: Both parents must cooperate, so the child will not grow up deprived of one parent. Young children and infants need frequent contact with both parents. Several times a week, even for short visits, is better for the young child than longer periods in between visits. Nursing should be allowed to continue. Even though it is difficult for parents to let go, it is necessary for the child's sake to let the child establish a relationship with the other parent. The consequences are far worse if they don't.

12. Parents say their children need only one home

Concepts: After separation and divorce children need a home with each parent. A child's security lies in having continuing close relationship with both parents.

13. A parent is living with another man or woman

Concepts: No matter what your own view of people living together might be, each person has the right to decide about this for him or herself. Parents each also have the right to share their lives and loved ones with their children, unless of course it can be shown to be detrimental.

14. A parent is unreliable and visits are sporadic

Stress importance of keeping promises to the children.

Concepts: Children suffer greatly when a parent comes late or doesn't come at all. Loving and trusting go together.

Adapted from <u>Child Custody Mediation</u> by Florence Bienenfeld, Ph.D., 1stBooks Library, 2002, 1-888-280-7715 or www.1stbooks.com or Amazon.com

<u>Appendix XI</u>

CREATING A CLOSER RELATIONSHIP WITH YOUR CHILD

To help your child do well in life, the best gift you can give him or her is a close, loving relationship. The twelve guidelines below can help you achieve this closeness and make your child feel loved.

1. *Become a good listener.* Even if you don't agree with what your child is saying, be willing to listen without interrupting and then discuss the problem afterward. This will enable your child to feel he or she can talk to you.

2. *Allow your child to express feelings,* even hostile, angry feelings, and allow him or her to cry. This will help your child feel comfortable around you.

3. *Comfort and reassure your child* when he or she is upset. This will establish feelings of security and of being loved by you.

4. *Be demonstrative — show your affection for your child.* Be free with your hugs and kisses and, whenever appropriate, tell your child that you love him or her. This will establish a loving closeness between you.

5. *Protect your child from parental disputes or disagreements.* If you involve the child, it will make him or her feel insecure and uncomfortable around you.

6. *Set reasonable rules and limits for your child's behavior according to his or her age and development.* In time this will help him or her to see you as fair and reasonable. It is not unusual for young children to have temper tantrums when they don't get their way. Allow them to cry, kick, or scream

without being punished or given their way. Gradually, your child will learn your rules and what behavior you expect.

7. *Along with discipline, give your child as much praise as you can.* Your child will grow up feeling good about herself or himself. Avoid corporal punishment of any kind: slapping, grabbing, hitting, beating, shaking, choking, or any other action that might make your child fear you. Harsh punishment can weaken your child's ego and destroy your chances for a close relationship. Avoid threatening to punish your child or to send her or him away. Also avoid prolonged punishments, such as long periods of being grounded or deprived of privileges.

8. *Do not call your child names or use put-downs.* These can cause a child to feel unloved, uneasy, and insecure. It may also make him or her overly sensitive and spoil his or her capacity to develop friendships.

9. *Set realistic goals for your child,* and try not to have unrealistic expectations based on what *you* wanted out of life. Do not make your child feel guilty about disappointing you, for this could make him or her feel like a bad person and uncomfortable or sad in your presence.

10. *Avoid excessive behavior around your child,* especially drug use and alcohol abuse. If you have a drinking or drug abuse problem, be honest with yourself about it and get help. Children become very frightened when parents are out of control. Your child will dread being around you and eventually will not want to see you at all.

11. *Take time to play with your child.* Choose activities geared to your child's age and interests. Children enjoy a wide variety of activities: picnics, walks, biking, games, cooking. There are also inexpensive places to take children, such as parks, beaches, the zoo, or museums, and occasionally including one

of your child's friends can increase the enjoyment. For young children, avoid activities that involve long periods of sitting.

12. *Gradually, patiently, and with love, help your child to learn and grow in knowledge, skills, and independence.* The better your child feels about himself or herself, the better he or she will feel about you.

Excerpts from <u>Helping Your Child Through Your Divorce</u> by Florence Bienenfeld, Ph.D., Hunter House, 1995, 1-800-266-5592 or www.HunterHouse.com or Amazon.com

Other Books by Author

Child Custody Mediation: Techniques for Mediators, Judges, Attorneys, Counselors and Parents, 1stBooks, 2002, 1-888-280-7715 or www.1stbooks.com or Amazon.com

Helping Your Child Through Your Divorce, Hunter House, Inc., 1995, 1-800-266-5592 or www.HunterHouse.com or Amazon.com

Do-It-Yourself Conflict Resolution for Couples, Career Press, 2000, 1-800-CAREER-1 or www.CareerPress.com or Amazon.com

About the Author

Dr. Florence Bienenfeld has been a Marriage, Family and Child Counselor for over 30 years and served as a Senior Family Counselor and Mediator for the Conciliation Court of Los Angeles County for 11 years. She has counseled thousands of families and is the author of <u>My Mom and Dad Are Getting a Divorce</u>, a healing book about divorce for children 4 to 12 and their parents (1stBooks, 2002); <u>Child Custody Mediation: Techniques for Mediators, Judges, Attorneys, Counselors and Parents</u> (1stBooks, 2002); <u>Helping Your Child Through Your Divorce</u>, a complete guide to helping children deal with divorce (Hunter House, Inc., 1995); and <u>Do-It-Yourself Conflict Resolution for Couples</u>, a dynamic couple's guide for resolving disagreements amicably, clearing away resentments and healing troubled relationships (Career Press, 2000).

Dr. Bienenfeld has written numerous articles for professional journals and has appeared as guest expert on radio and television. In 1987 to 1988, she was commissioned to write a Parent Education Manual for Family Court Services of California, Administrative Office of the Court. Florence is a clinical member of the American Association of Marriage and Family Therapists, California Association of Marriage and Family Therapists, American Society of Clinical Hypnosis, Southern California Society of Clinical Hypnosis and was recipient of awards for outstanding service to families and children of divorce from Association of Family Conciliation Courts in 1980 and 1985; from Mayor of the City of Santa Monica and from the County of Los Angeles in 1985; and the Clark Vincent Award from California Association of Marriage and Family Therapists for Outstanding Literary Contributions to the Profession in 1990.

Presently, Dr. Bienenfeld is in private practice in Pacific Palisades, California specializing in Short-Term Therapy, Couple and Family Mediation, and Child-Custody Mediation.

27526127R00071

Made in the USA
San Bernardino, CA
13 December 2015